Ace Your Math Test

ADDITION AND SUBTRACTION

Ace your Math Test

Rebecca Wingard-Nelson

 Enslow Publishers, Inc.
40 Industrial Road
Box 398
Berkeley Heights, NJ 07922
USA

http://www.enslow.com

Library of Congress Cataloging-in-Publication Data
Wingard-Nelson, Rebecca.
  Addition and subtraction / Rebecca Wingard-Nelson.
    p. cm. — (Ace your math test)
  Includes index.
  Summary: "Learn how to add and subtract whole numbers, decimals, fractions, measurements, and about regrouping numbers, mental math, and estimation"—Provided by publisher.
  ISBN 978-0-7660-3778-6
  1. Addition—Juvenile literature. 2. Subtraction—Juvenile literature. I. Title.
  QA115.W74 2011
  513.2'11—dc22
                              2011002100

Paperback ISBN 978-1-4644-0005-6
ePUB ISBN 978-1-4645-0453-2
PDF ISBN 978-1-4646-0453-9

Printed in the United States of America

092011 Lake Book Manufacturing, Inc., Melrose Park, IL

10 9 8 7 6 5 4 3 2 1

To Our Readers: We have done our best to make sure all Internet Addresses in this book were active and appropriate when we went to press. However, the author and the publisher have no control over and assume no liability for the material available on those Internet sites or on other Web sites they may link to. Any comments or suggestions can be sent by e-mail to comments@enslow.com or to the address on the back cover.

♻ Enslow Publishers, Inc., is committed to printing our books on recycled paper. The paper in every book contains 10% to 30% post-consumer waste (PCW). The cover board on the outside of each book contains 100% PCW. Our goal is to do our part to help young people and the environment too!

Illustration Credits: Shutterstock.com

Cover Photo: © iStockphoto.com/Jacom Stephens

CONTENTS

Test-Taking Tips

Be Prepared!

Most of the topics that are found on math tests are taught in the classroom. Paying attention in class, taking good notes, and keeping up with your homework are the best ways to be prepared for tests.

Practice

Use test preparation materials, such as flash cards and timed worksheets, to practice your basic math skills. Take practice tests. They show the kinds of items that will be on the actual test. They can show you what areas you understand, and what areas you need more practice in.

Test Day!

The Night Before

Relax. Eat a good meal. Go to bed early enough to get a good night's sleep. Don't cram on new material! Review the material you know is going to be on the test.

Get what you need ready. Sharpen your pencils, and set out things like erasers, a calculator, and any extra materials, like books, protractors, tissues, or cough drops.

The Big Day

Get up early enough to eat breakfast and not have to hurry. Wear something that is comfortable and makes you feel good. Listen to your favorite music.

Get to school and class on time. Stay calm. Stay positive.

Test Time!

Before you begin, take a deep breath. Focus on the test, not the people or things around you. Remind yourself to do your best and not worry about what you do not know.

Work through the entire test, but don't spend too much time on any one problem. Don't rush, but move quickly, answering all of the questions you can do easily. Go back a second time and answer the questions that take more time.

Read each question completely. Read all the answer choices. Eliminate answers that are obviously wrong. Read word problems carefully, and decide what the problem is asking.

Check each answer to make sure it is reasonable. Estimate numbers to see if your answer makes sense.

Concentrate on the test. Stay focused. If your attention starts to wander, take a short break. Breathe. Relax. Refocus. Don't get upset if you can't answer a question. Mark it, then come back to it later.

When you finish, look back over the entire test. Are all of the questions answered? Check as many problems as you can. Look at your calculations and make sure you have the same answer on the blank as you do on your worksheet.

Let's Go!

Three common types of test problems are covered in this book: Multiple Choice, Show Your Work, and Explain Your Answer. Tips on how to solve each, as well as common errors to avoid, are also presented. Knowing what to expect on a test and what is expected of you will have you ready to ace every math test you take.

1. Whole Number Addition

Definitions

addend: The number that is being added.

sum: The answer in an addition problem.

Count Up

Stephanie played 4 video games before dinner. Later that night, she played 3 more video games. How many video games did Stephanie play in all?

Step 1: One way to add is to using counting. Start with the first number. Stephanie played 4 video games.

4

Step 2: Stephanie played 3 more video games.
Start with 4, then count up 3 more.

4, 5, 6, 7

Stephanie played 7 video games in all.

TEST TIME: Multiple Choice

What is the sum of 6 and 2?

          a. 5

          b. 6

          c. 7

          (d.) 8

A sum is a total, or the answer to an addition problem.
Add 6 and 2. You can add by counting up 2 more from 6.
You could also use a drawing or use items, such as your fingers,
to add. Draw 6 and 2. Count to find the total.

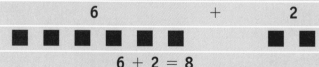

$$6 + 2 = 8$$

Solution: The correct answer is d.

Test-Taking Hint

Multiple choice questions give you a set of answers.
You choose which of the given answers is correct.

Know the Facts

Addition is the basis of all of the other operations.
Subtraction is the opposite of addition.
Multiplication is repeated addition.
Division is repeated subtraction.

What are the addition facts up to 5 for 3s?

Step 1: The problem is asking you to show all the addition facts that add 3 and 0, 1, 2, 3, 4, and 5. Write each problem.

$3 + 0 =$ $3 + 1 =$ $3 + 2 =$

$3 + 3 =$ $3 + 4 =$ $3 + 5 =$

Step 2: Find the sum for each addition fact.

$3 + 0 = 3$ $3 + 1 = 4$ $3 + 2 = 5$

$3 + 3 = 6$ $3 + 4 = 7$ $3 + 5 = 8$

Memorize the addition facts for the numbers 0 to 10. Knowing the facts will make test taking fast and easy.

Test-Taking Hint

Some problems ask a question and ask you to explain your answer. Others just ask for an explanation. Your score is based on both a correct response and how clearly you explain your reasoning.

TEST TIME: Explain Your Answer

Chris made a stash of 7 snowballs to throw at his brother. While he hid behind a tree and waited, he made 3 more. How many snowballs did Chris make? How did you decide?

Solution: This problem starts with some snowballs, then more are added. Start with the number Chris made first. Add the number he made while hiding.

$$7 + 3 = 10$$

Chris made 10 snowballs.

Problems that use words like increase, more, sum, or combined may be addition problems. Addition problems take two or more values and combine them.

2. Greater Number Addition

Place Value

Add 12 + 32

Step 1: Adding numbers that have more than one digit is done using place value. Line up the numbers in a column by their place value.

```
    tens ones
     12
   + 32
```

Step 2: Add each place value from right to left. Add the ones.

```
     12
   + 32
   ────
      4
```

Step 3: Add the tens.

```
     12
   + 32
   ────
     44
```

12 + 32 = 44

TEST TIME: Show Your Work

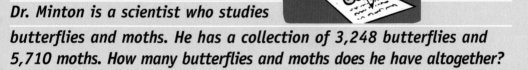

Dr. Minton is a scientist who studies butterflies and moths. He has a collection of 3,248 butterflies and 5,710 moths. How many butterflies and moths does he have altogether?

This is an addition problem. You can add any size numbers using place value. Line up the numbers by place value. Add each place, beginning on the right with the ones place.

Solution:

$$\begin{array}{r} 3{,}248 \\ +\ 5{,}710 \\ \hline 8{,}958 \end{array}$$

Dr. Minton has 8,958 butterflies and moths.

Test-Taking Hint

Questions that ask you to show how you found the solution are sometimes called "Show Your Work" or "Short Answer" questions. Showing your work and showing some effort will earn you part of the credit, even if you have the wrong answer. The right answer, without showing some work, may only give you partial credit.

Different Digits

Add 3,821 + 74

Step 1: When the addends have a different number of digits, be very careful to line up the place values.

$$
\begin{array}{r}
3,821 \\
+\quad 74 \\
\hline
\end{array}
$$

Step 2: Add each place value from right to left. Add the ones, then tens, then hundreds, then thousands.

$$
\begin{array}{r}
3,821 \\
+\quad 74 \\
\hline
3,895
\end{array}
$$

$3,821 + 74 = 3,895$

TEST TIME: Multiple Choice

Michael has 12 blue T-shirts, 5 red T-shirts, and 20 black T-shirts. How many T-shirts does Michael have in all?

a. 19
b. 32
c. 37
d. 82

Addition problems with more than two addends	12
are added using place value. Line up the numbers	5
by place value. Add each place, beginning on the	+ 20
right with the ones place.	37

Solution: The correct answer is c.

3. Regrouping

Basic Facts

Some of the basic addition facts have two-digit sums.

What is 8 + 3?

Step 1: Use a drawing to help you understand the addition.

Step 2: Combine the two sets of circles. Count the combined number.

Step 3: When you write the problem in a column, you see that the sum is a two-digit number. The sum carries over into the tens column. When the sum of a column carries into the next column, it is called regrouping. You can regroup 11 ones as 1 ten and 1 one.

$$\begin{array}{r} 8 \\ + \ 3 \\ \hline 11 \end{array}$$

TEST TIME: Multiple Choice

Anita has 5 cats. One of her cats had 7 kittens.
How many cats does Anita have now?

        a. 5
        b. 7
        c. 10
       (d.) 12

Anita started with 5 cats. Then she added 7 more. This is an addition problem. You can eliminate answers a and b by understanding that they are the addends, and the sum must be larger than either addend. Add 5 + 7 = 12.

Solution: Anita has 12 cats now. Answer d is correct.

Test-Taking Hint

Read problems carefully. Decide how you can use the information given to solve the problem.

Definition

regrouping: Using place value to rename values. For example: 20 ones can be regrouped as **2** tens, and 10 tens can be regrouped as 1 hundred.

More Addends

Add 7 + 9 + 5

Step 1: Use a drawing to help you understand the addition.

7	+	9	+	5

● ● ● ●   ● ● ● ● ●   ● ● ●
● ● ●   ● ● ● ●   ● ●

Step 2: Count the total number of circles.

7 + 9 + 5 = 21

● ● ● ● ● ● ● ● ● ● ●
● ● ● ● ● ● ● ● ● ●

Step 3: In this problem, 2 tens are regrouped. This regrouping is sometimes called carrying. In this problem, 2 tens are carried from the ones to the tens place.

$$\begin{array}{r} 7 \\ 9 \\ +\ 5 \\ \hline 21 \end{array}$$

TEST TIME: Show Your Work

There are 9 people who have jobs in an office. Next week 9 more people are starting new jobs in the same office. No people are leaving. How many people in all will have jobs at the office?

There were 9 people who had jobs. Next week there will be 9 more. This is an addition problem.

For a problem that uses the basic fact, write out the fact. Then write the answer in a full sentence.

Solution: 9 + 9 = 18

In all, 18 people will have jobs at the office.

4. Multi-digit Regrouping

Regrouping

Add 36 + 15

Step 1: Line up the numbers in a column by their place value.

$$
\begin{array}{r}
36 \\
+\ 15 \\
\end{array}
$$

Step 2: Add the ones. 6 + 5 = 11. Regroup 11 ones as 1 ten and 1 one. Write the 1 ten above the tens column.

$$
\begin{array}{r}
1 \\
36 \\
+\ 15 \\
\hline
1 \\
\end{array}
$$

Step 3: Add the tens. Remember to add the 1 that was regrouped from the ones.

$$
\begin{array}{r}
1 \\
36 \\
+\ 15 \\
\hline
51 \\
\end{array}
$$

TEST TIME: Explain Your Answer

What does regrouping do in an addition problem? Give examples.

Solution: In addition, values in each place are combined. When the combined value in one of the places is greater than 9, the sum is regrouped into the next larger place.

For example, $6 + 6 = 12$. The 12 is 12 ones, or 1 ten and 2 ones. The 10 ones are regrouped as 1 ten.

Other places also regroup. Some examples are:

10 tens are regrouped as 1 hundred.

10 hundreds are regrouped as 1 thousand.

10 thousands are regrouped as 1 ten thousand.

10 ten thousands are regrouped as 1 hundred thousand.

Regrouping More than Once

Add 1,264 + 809

Step 1: Line up the numbers in a column.

$$\begin{array}{r} 1,264 \\ +809 \\ \hline \end{array}$$

Step 2: Add the ones. $4 + 9 = 13$. Regroup 13 ones as 1 ten and 3 ones. Write the 1 ten above the tens column.

$$\begin{array}{r} 1 \\ 1,264 \\ +809 \\ \hline 3 \end{array}$$

Step 3: Add the tens. $6 + 0 = 6$. Remember to add the 1 that was regrouped from the ones.

$$\begin{array}{r} 1 \\ 1,264 \\ +809 \\ \hline 73 \end{array}$$

Step 4: Add the hundreds. $2 + 8 = 10$. Regroup 10 hundreds as 1 thousand and 0 hundreds. Write the 1 thousand above the thousands place.

$$\begin{array}{r} 11 \\ 1,264 \\ +809 \\ \hline 073 \end{array}$$

Step 5: There is only one digit in the thousands place. Add the regrouped thousand to the thousands place.

$$\begin{array}{r} 11 \\ 1,264 \\ +809 \\ \hline 2,073 \end{array}$$

$1,264 + 809 = 2,073$

TEST TIME: Multiple Choice

Which of the following has a sum of 1,253?

> **a.** 672 + 581
> **b.** 328 + 925
> **c.** 804 + 449
> **d.** All of the above

Find the sum for each expression. Remember to add any regrouped digits to the next place value.

$$672 + 581 = 1,253$$
$$328 + 925 = 1,253$$
$$804 + 449 = 1,253$$

Solution: Since answers a, b, and c are all correct, the correct choice is answer d.

Test-Taking Hint

In multiple choice problems with the answer choice all of the above, it is best to check all of the choices.

5. Addition Properties

The Commutative Property

Changing the order of the addends in an addition problem does not change the sum.

Show that 30 + 12 has the same value as 12 + 30.

Step 1: Find the value of the first expression.
Write the addends in a column. Add.

$$
\begin{array}{r}
30 \\
+\ 12 \\
\hline
42
\end{array}
$$

Step 2: Find the value of the second expression.
Write the addends in a column. Add.

$$
\begin{array}{r}
12 \\
+\ 30 \\
\hline
42
\end{array}
$$

Step 3: Compare the sums.

$$30 + 12 = 42 \text{ and } 12 + 30 = 42$$

The order of the addends is changed, but the sums are the same.

TEST TIME: Multiple Choice

Kari had three bags of rice.
The bag weights were 25 pounds, 16 pounds, and 4 pounds.
How many pounds of rice did Kari have in all?

   a. 35 pounds
   b. 41 pounds
   c. 45 pounds
   d. 51 pounds

Add the weight in pounds for each bag. $25 + 16 + 4$

The Associative Property says that you can change the grouping of how you add numbers. Instead of adding the first two numbers first, add the last two numbers first. This combines 16 and 4 for a total of 20. Multiples and powers of ten are easy to add because they end in zeros.

$25 + (16 + 4) = 25 + 20 = 45$

Solution: Answer c is correct.

The Zero Property

Add 345 + 0

Step 1: Adding zero to any number does not change the value of the number.

$$345 + 0 = 345$$

TEST TIME: Multiple Choice

Which of the following illustrates the Commutative Property?

a. $6 + (3 + 5) = (6 + 3) + 5$
b. $27 + 35 = 35 + 27$
c. $0 + 12 = 12$
d. $18 + 32 = 6 + 12 + 32$

The Commutative Property says changing the order of the addends does not change the sum. Answers a and b show how addends can be moved or grouped and have the same value. Answer a keeps the same order, but groups the addends differently. Answer b changes the order of the addends.

Solution: The correct answer is b.

TEST TIME: Explain Your Answer

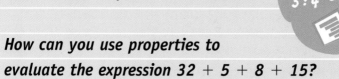

How can you use properties to
evaluate the expression 32 + 5 + 8 + 15?

Solution: Use the Commutative Property to change the order of
the addends. Move addends together that will have a sum that
is a multiple of ten. 32 and 8 have a 2 and 8 in the ones places,
which total 10. The 5 and 15 have 5 and 5 in the ones place, which
total 10.

$$32 + 5 + 8 + 15 = 32 + 8 + 5 + 15$$

Use the Associative Property to group the addends.

$$32 + 8 + 5 + 15 = (32 + 8) + (5 + 15)$$

Add the grouped addends mentally, then add again.

$$(32 + 8) + (5 + 15) = (40) + (20) = 60$$

Test-Taking Hint

Knowing the properties can make solving addition problems
easier. Be careful to only apply the addition properties to
addition, since they are NOT all true for subtraction.

6. Whole Number Subtraction

Definitions

minuend: The number you subtract from in a subtraction problem.

subtrahend: The number you subtract in a subtraction problem.

difference: The answer to a subtraction problem.

minuend − subtrahend = difference

Basic Subtraction

Subtract 8 − 2

Step 1: Subtraction problems start with a value, then take part of it away. Start with 8. This is the minuend.

Step 2: Take 2 away. This is the subtrahend.

Step 3: The number left, 6, is the difference.

8 − 2 = 6

TEST TIME: Show Your Work

Horace had 14 baby guppies. He gave
9 of them to a pet store. How many baby guppies does
Horace have left?

Horace had some baby guppies, then he gave some away.
This is a subtraction problem.

For a problem that uses a basic fact, write out the fact.
Then write the answer in a full sentence.

Solution: $14 - 9 = 5$

Horace has 5 baby guppies left.

Test-Taking Hint

Problems that use words like left, difference, remain, fewer,
or less may be subtraction problems. Subtraction problems
start with a value, then take some of the value away.

TEST TIME: Multiple Choice

Which of the following is NOT a reason to use subtraction?

a. To find the difference between two values
b. To find the remainder when part of a value is taken away
c. To find the total when two parts are given
d. To find the other part when the total and one part are known

This problem asks you to decide which is NOT a reason to use subtraction.

a. You can use subtraction to find a difference. The difference between 6 and 2 is 4. $6 - 2 = 4$
b. You can use subtraction to find what remains. If you have $7 and spend $1, you have $7 - $1 = $6 remaining.
c. To find the total of two parts, you use addition.
d. You can use subtraction to find the other part of a total when one part is known. If you have 9 students, and 6 are boys, then $9 - 6 = 3$ are girls.

Solution: The correct answer is c.

Subtracting Zero

Subtract 6 − 0

Step 1: Subtract.

$$6 - 0 = 6$$

Subtract 571 − 0

Step 1: Subtracting zero from any number, no matter the size, does not change the value of the number.

$$571 - 0 = 571$$

Test-Taking Hint

Not all of the questions on a math test need computations. Know math definitions and know the reasons behind the math.

7. Inverse Operations

Addition and Subtraction

Inverse operations do the opposite of each other. Addition and subtraction are inverse operations.

Mikayla said that 27 − 15 = 12.
Use addition to check her answer.

Step 1: Opposite, or inverse, operations can be used to check answers. For the problem above, add the answer, 12, and the number that was subtracted, 15.

$$12 + 15 = 27$$

Step 2: Compare the sum and the original minuend, 27. They are the same.

Mikayla's answer is correct.

Test-Taking Hint

Read all problems carefully. Even the simplest problems can be answered incorrectly when they are not read correctly. The problem on page 31 asks you to check the answer. If you do NOT include checking the answer, the solution is not complete.

TEST TIME: Show Your Work

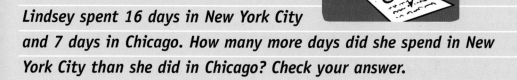

Lindsey spent 16 days in New York City and 7 days in Chicago. How many more days did she spend in New York City than she did in Chicago? Check your answer.

This problem asks you to compare two numbers by finding the difference. It is a subtraction problem.

Solution: 16 days − 7 days = 9 days

Lindsey spent 9 days more in New York City than she did in Chicago.

Think about this problem. Your answer says that Lindsey spent 9 more than 7 days in New York City. Use addition to check.

9 + 7 = 16 Correct.

Addition and Subtraction

What is the fact family that includes 1 + 5 = 6?

Step 1: For every addition fact, there is a related subtraction fact. Addition combines 1 and 5 into 6. Subtraction starts with 6 and takes 5 away, leaving 1. When you know $1 + 5 = 6$, you also know $6 - 5 = 1$.

$$1 + 5 = 6 \qquad 6 - 5 = 1$$

Step 2: The Commutative Property tells you that since $1 + 5 = 6$, then $5 + 1 = 6$. The related subtraction fact for $5 + 1 = 6$ is $6 - 1 = 5$.

$$5 + 1 = 6 \qquad 6 - 1 = 5$$

Step 3: The four related facts are sometimes called a fact family. Write them together.

$$1 + 5 = 6 \qquad 6 - 5 = 1$$
$$5 + 1 = 6 \qquad 6 - 1 = 5$$

TEST TIME: Multiple Choice

What is the missing number in this fact family?

$$6 + \_\_ = 13 \qquad \_\_ + 6 = 13$$
$$13 - \_\_ = 6 \qquad 13 - 6 = \_\_$$

a. 5
b. 6
c. 7
d. 8

You can use any of the four facts to find the missing number. In each fact, the missing number is 7.

Solution: The correct answer is c.

Test-Taking Hint

When a question is taking an especially long time or has you stumped, leave it and go on. Come back later if you have time.

8. Subtracting Larger Numbers

Place Value

Subtract 85 − 61

Step 1: Write the problem in a column. Line up the digits with the same place values.

$$
\begin{array}{r}
\text{tens ones} \\
85 \\
-\ 61 \\
\hline
\end{array}
$$

Step 2: Subtract each place value from right to left. Subtract the ones.

$$
\begin{array}{r}
85 \\
-\ 61 \\
\hline
4
\end{array}
$$

Step 3: Subtract the tens.

$$
\begin{array}{r}
85 \\
-\ 61 \\
\hline
24
\end{array}
$$

$85 - 61 = 24$

TEST TIME: Multiple Choice

Which of the following is NOT correct?

a. 68 − 22 = 46
ⓑ 37 − 16 = 11
c. 95 − 70 = 25
d. 44 − 42 = 2

This problem asks you to find the equation that is not correct.
Three of the four ARE correct.

One way to solve this problem is to solve each equation.
Remember, you are looking for the equation that is NOT correct.

a. 68	b. 37	c. 95	d. 44
− 22	− 16	− 70	− 42
46	21	25	2

Solution: The only equation that is not correct is in answer b.

Greater Numbers

Subtract 68,745 − 4,035

Step 1: Numbers of any size can be subtracted using place value. Line up the digits.

$$\begin{array}{r} 68{,}745 \\ -\ 4{,}035 \\ \hline \end{array}$$

Step 2: Subtract from right to left. Subtract ones.

$$\begin{array}{r} 68{,}745 \\ -\ 4{,}035 \\ \hline 0 \end{array}$$

Step 3: Subtract tens.

$$\begin{array}{r} 68{,}745 \\ -\ 4{,}035 \\ \hline 10 \end{array}$$

Step 4: Subtract hundreds.

$$\begin{array}{r} 68{,}745 \\ -\ 4{,}035 \\ \hline 710 \end{array}$$

Step 5: Subtract thousands.

$$\begin{array}{r} 68{,}745 \\ -\ 4{,}035 \\ \hline 4{,}710 \end{array}$$

Step 6: Subtract ten thousands.

$$\begin{array}{r} 68{,}745 \\ -\ 4{,}035 \\ \hline 64{,}710 \end{array}$$

$68{,}745 - 4{,}035 = 64{,}710$

TEST TIME: Show Your Work

A large classroom has a floor area of 27,584 square feet. A 5,200-square-foot area has carpet. The rest is covered in tile. How much area of the room is covered in tile?

This problem tells you the whole area. It gives you part of the area and asks you to find the other part. It is a subtraction problem.

Solution:

Total area − carpet area = tile area

27,584 sq ft − 5,200 sq ft = tile area

$$
\begin{array}{r}
27{,}584 \\
-\ 5{,}200 \\
\hline
22{,}384 \text{ sq ft}
\end{array}
\qquad
\begin{array}{r}
\text{Check:}\quad 22{,}384 \\
+\ 5{,}200 \\
\hline
27{,}584
\end{array}
$$

The room has 22,384 square feet of tiled area.

Test-Taking Hint

Word problems, or story problems, should be answered in complete sentences.

9. Subtraction Regrouping

Borrowing

Subtract 21 − 9

Step 1: Use a drawing to help you understand subtraction. Let's use a bar to represent a ten, and a circle to represent a one. Begin by drawing 21.

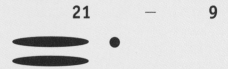

Step 2: To subtract 9, you need to have 9 ones. Since there are not 9 ones, regroup 1 ten as ten ones. This regrouping is sometimes called borrowing. This problem borrows 1 from the tens place.

Step 3: Show subtraction by crossing off 9 ones.

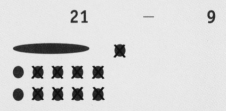

Step 4: Count the values that are left. This is the difference.

$$21 \quad - \quad 9 \quad = \quad 12$$

TEST TIME: Explain Your Answer

What does regrouping do in a subtraction problem? Give examples.

Solution: In subtraction, greater place values are regrouped to smaller ones. When the digit being subtacted is greater than the digit being taken from, you can regroup from the next larger place.

For example, in the problem 22 − 8 = 14, the digit being subtracted in the ones place is an 8. The digit it is being taken from is a 2. Since 8 is greater than 2, regroup 1 ten as 10 ones. This gives you 12 ones. Now you can subtract 8 ones from 12 ones.

Other places also regroup. Some examples are:

1 hundred is regrouped as 10 tens

1 thousand is regrouped as 10 hundreds

1 ten thousand is regrouped as 10 thousands

Regrouping in Subtraction

Subtract 24 − 16

Step 1: Write the problem in a column.
Line up the digits with the same place values.

$$\begin{array}{r} 24 \\ -\ 16 \\ \hline \end{array}$$

Step 2: Subtract each place value from right to left. Look at the ones column. You cannot subtract 6 ones from 4 ones.

Regroup 2 tens and 4 ones
as 1 ten and 14 ones.

$$\begin{array}{r} {}^{1}14 \\ \cancel{2}\cancel{4} \\ -\ 16 \\ \hline \end{array}$$

Step 3: Subtract the ones.

$$\begin{array}{r} {}^{1}14 \\ \cancel{2}\cancel{4} \\ -\ 16 \\ \hline 8 \end{array}$$

Step 3: Subtract the tens.

$$\begin{array}{r} {}^{1}14 \\ \cancel{2}\cancel{4} \\ -\ 16 \\ \hline 8 \end{array}$$

24 − 16 = 8

TEST TIME: Show Your Work

Ronda lives in Athens, a small town
with a population of only 92 people. There are 27 children and
36 dogs. How many adults live in Athens?

This problem tells you a whole amount, the population, and part
of the amount, 27 children. It asks for the other part, the adults.
This is a subtraction problem.

Solution:

Population − children = adults

92 − 27 = adults

$$
\begin{array}{r}
^{8\ 12} \\
\cancel{9}\cancel{2} \\
-\ 27 \\
\hline
65
\end{array}
\qquad
\text{Check:}
\begin{array}{r}
^{1} \\
65 \\
+\ 27 \\
\hline
92
\end{array}
$$

There are 65 adults that live in Athens.

Test-Taking Hint

Word problems sometimes include extra information
to distract you. The problem above gives the number of
dogs in Athens, but you don't need to know this.

10. More Regrouping

Regrouping Hundreds

Subtract 528 − 374

Step 1: Write the problem in a column.
Line up the digits with the same place values.

$$528$$
$$-\ 374$$

Step 2: Subtract each place value from right to left. Subtract the ones.

$$528$$
$$-\ 374$$
$$\overline{4}$$

Step 3: Look at the tens column.
You cannot subtract 7 tens from 2 tens.

Regroup 5 hundreds as 4 hundreds and 10 tens.

$$\overset{4\ 12}{\cancel{5}28}$$
$$-\ 374$$
$$\overline{4}$$

Step 4: Subtract the tens.

$$\overset{4\ 12}{\cancel{5}28}$$
$$-\ 374$$
$$\overline{54}$$

Step 5: Subtract the hundreds.

$$\overset{4\ 12}{\cancel{5}28}$$
$$-\ 374$$
$$\overline{154}$$

$$528 - 374 = 154$$

TEST TIME: Show Your Work

Subtract 265 from 6,197

This problem uses the words *subtract* and *from*. This means you should begin with the second value, 6,197, and subtract the first value, 265.

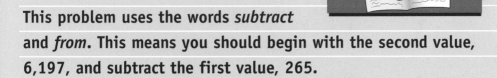

Solution:

```
        5 11
        6̸,1̸97
      −  265
        5,932
```

Check:

```
          1
        5,932
      +  265
        6,197
```

6,197 − 265 = 5,932

A computer store is having a tag sale. Red tagged computers are on sale for $199. Blue tagged computers are on sale for $327. What is the difference in price?

       (a.) $128
       b. $138
       c. $228
       d. $238

Subtract the lower price from the higher price to find the difference.

For this problem, you need to regroup for more than one place value.

First, regroup 2 tens as 1 ten and 10 ones.

Then, regroup 3 hundreds as 2 hundreds and 10 tens.

$$\begin{array}{r} {}^{2}\cancel{3}{}^{1}\cancel{2}7 \\ 327 \\ -\ 199 \\ \hline 128 \end{array}$$

Solution: The correct answer is a.

Test-Taking Hint

Put a small mark next to answers you're not sure of, or do not finish. When you finish your test, go back to those problems.

Subtraction Across Zeros

Subtract 1,000 − 498

Step 1: Write the problem in a column.
Line up the digits with the same place values.

$$\begin{array}{r} 1{,}000 \\ -\ 498 \\ \hline \end{array}$$

Step 2: When there are zeros in the minuend, you may need to regroup in more than one place. To subtract ones, you must regroup. There are no tens or hundreds to regroup. Regroup 1 thousand as 10 hundreds.

$$\begin{array}{r} 10 \\ \cancel{1}{,}000 \\ -\ 498 \\ \hline \end{array}$$

Step 3: Regroup 10 hundreds as 9 hundreds and 10 tens.

$$\begin{array}{r} 9 \\ \cancel{10}10 \\ \cancel{1}{,}\cancel{0}00 \\ -\ 498 \\ \hline \end{array}$$

Step 4: Regroup 10 tens as 9 tens and 10 ones.

$$\begin{array}{r} 99 \\ \cancel{10}\cancel{10}10 \\ \cancel{1}{,}\cancel{0}\cancel{0}0 \\ -\ 498 \\ \hline \end{array}$$

Step 5: Subtract.

$$\begin{array}{r} 99 \\ \cancel{10}\cancel{10}10 \\ \cancel{1}{,}\cancel{0}\cancel{0}\cancel{0} \\ -\ 498 \\ \hline 502 \end{array}$$

1,000 − 498 = 502

11. Mental Math: Addition

Definition

multiple of ten: The result of 10 multiplied by another number. An example of a multiple of ten is 80, because $10 \times 8 = 80$. Multiples of ten end in at least one zero.

Multiples of Ten

Add 90 + 70

Step 1: Addends that have only one digit other than zero can be added mentally. When that digit has the same place value in each addend, add that place value.

90 is the same as 9 tens.
70 is the same as 7 tens.

$90 + 70 = 160$

$$\begin{array}{r} 9 \text{ tens} \\ + \ 7 \text{ tens} \\ \hline 16 \text{ tens or } 160 \end{array}$$

Add 300 + 200

Step 1: Add only the hundreds place.

300 is the same as 3 hundreds.
200 is the same as 2 hundreds.

$300 + 200 = 500$

$$\begin{array}{r} 3 \text{ hundreds} \\ + \ 2 \text{ hundreds} \\ \hline 5 \text{ hundreds} \end{array}$$

TEST TIME: Multiple Choice

Add 500 + 30,000 + 1,000 + 8 + 20

   a. 31,258
   b. 31,528
   c. 30,708
   d. 35,128

When each addend has only one digit that is not zero, you can use mental math. In this problem, each of the non-zero digits has a different place value. Each non-zero digit from the addends will appear in the answer. Watch what happens when you line up the addends in a column to add.

$$
\begin{array}{r}
500 \\
30,000 \\
1,000 \\
8 \\
+20 \\
\hline
31,528 \\
\end{array}
$$

Solution: The correct answer is b.

TEST TIME: Explain Your Answer

*Alisha cut 32-inch-long strings
to make friendship bracelets.
She has 6 gold strings, 8 blue strings, 2 black strings, and 4 white
strings. How can you use mental math to find the total number
of strings Alisha cut?*

Solution:

Alisha cut these numbers of strings:

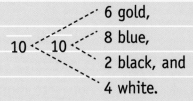

6 gold,

8 blue,

2 black, and

4 white.

You can group these strings easily into sets of 10. 6 and 4 are 10, and
8 and 2 are 10. There are 2 sets of 10, or 20 strings in all.

Alisha cut a total of 20 strings.

Test-Taking Hint

Pay more attention to the question you are working on
than to the amount of time left for the test.

Give and Take

Section A has 107 seats. Section B has 212 seats.
How many seats do the two sections have together?

Step 1: This problem gives you two amounts and asks for the total amount. It is an addition problem. Add the number of seats in each section.

107 + 212 = ____

Step 2: You can take part of one of the addends and give the same amount to the other.

Take 7 off of 107 to make it 100. 100 is easier to add than 107.

Step 3: You took 7 off 107, so give 7 to 212. 212 + 7 is easy because there is no regrouping.

212 + 7 = 219

Step 4: Add the two new numbers mentally.

100 + 219 = 319, so 107 + 212 = 319.

There are 319 seats in sections A and B together.

12. Mental Math: Subtraction

Count Up

Subtract 150 − 127 mentally.

Step 1: Sometimes it is easier to count up from the number you are subtracting to the number you are subtracting from, like counting up from 127 to 150. Count up ones to the nearest ten.

Start with 127. It takes 3 more to get to 130.

Step 2: Count up to the original number.

From 130 to 150 is 20.

Step 3: Add what you counted up.

3 + 20 = 23

Test-Taking Hint

When you don't feel confident about an answer, and have time, try solving it a different way. That way, you are less likely to make the same mistake twice.

TEST TIME: Multiple Choice

Robyn had $268. She bought a coat and scarf for $123. How much money does she have left?

   a. $145
   b. $148
   c. $168
   d. $191

You can break the amount being subtracted into smaller amounts to subtract mentally. $123 is the same as $100 + $20 + $3. Start with $268 and mentally subtract $100.

$268 − $100 = $168

Mentally subtract $20.

$168 − $20 = $148

Mentally subtract $3.

$148 − $3 = $145

Solution: The correct answer is a.

Nines

Nina's computer class has 26 computers for students to work on. Today, 9 of the computers are not working. How many computers are available for students to work on today?

Step 1: This problem gives you a total amount, 26 computers, and part of the total, 9 not working. You are asked to find the remaining number. This is a subtraction problem.

$$26 - 9 = \underline{\qquad}$$

Step 2: You can subtract 9 mentally by understanding that 9 is 1 less than 10. Think of subtracting 9 as taking away 10, then adding 1 back. Subtract 10.

$$26 - 10 = 16$$

Step 3: Add back 1.

$$16 + 1 = 17$$
$$26 - 9 = 17$$

There are 17 computers available today.

Test-Taking Hint

This also works for numbers that end in 9, like 19 or 29. For numbers that end in other digits like 7 or 8, you can think of 7 as 3 less than 10, and 8 as 2 less than 10.

Some problems can be answered in more than one way. You may use a different method to solve the same problem as someone else, and still have a correct answer.

TEST TIME: Explain Your Answer

Explain one way you can use mental math to find the difference between 415 and 196.

Solution:

In a subtraction problem, you can add the same amount to the subtrahend and minuend and the difference does not change. Look at these examples:

$5 - 2 = 3$	Add 1s	$6 - 3 = 3$	
$5 - 2 = 3$	Add 10s	$15 - 12 = 3$	

To find the difference between 415 and 196, you must subtract $415 - 196$. Numbers that end in zeros are easy to subtract. If you add 4 to 196, you get 200. Add 4 to both 415 and 196, then subtract.

$$415 - 196 = 419 - 200 = 219$$

13. Decimal Addition

Definition

decimal: A number based on ten. In a decimal, a decimal point separates whole number values from values less than one.

16.23
whole number.less than one

Place Value

Decimals have the same place value pattern as whole numbers. Each place has a value that is ten times the place on its right.

Add 1.7 and 0.2

Step 1: Write the numbers in a column. When the decimal points are lined up, the place values are also lined up.

$$\begin{array}{r} 1.7 \\ +\ 0.2 \\ \hline \end{array}$$

Step 2: Add the tenths. Write the decimal point in the answer.

$$\begin{array}{r} 1.7 \\ +\ 0.2 \\ \hline .9 \end{array}$$

Step 3: Add the ones.

$$\begin{array}{r} 1.7 \\ +\ 0.2 \\ \hline 1.9 \end{array}$$

$1.7 + 0.2 = 1.9$

TEST TIME: Multiple Choice

5.32 + 2.407 = _____

      a. 5.439

      b. 5.539

      c. 7.607

      (d.) 7.727

Write the numbers in a column. These numbers have a different number of digits on the right of the decimal point. Be very careful to add only digits that have the same place value. Line up the decimal points. You may use zeros as placeholders to write the addends.

$$
\begin{array}{r}
5.320 \\
+\ 2.407 \\
\hline
7.727
\end{array}
$$

Solution: The correct answer is d.

Adding Money

Add $12.74 and $26.38

Step 1: Money amounts are added like other decimals. Write the decimals in a column.

$$\begin{array}{r} \$12.74 \\ + \ \$26.38 \\ \hline \end{array}$$

Step 2: Add the digits in each place, beginning on the right. Decimal values are regrouped in the same way as whole numbers. 10 hundredths are regrouped as 1 tenth. 10 tenths are regrouped as 1 one.

$$\begin{array}{r} 1 \ 1 \quad \\ \$12.74 \\ + \ \$26.38 \\ \hline \$39.12 \end{array}$$

$12.74 + $26.38 = $39.12

Test-Taking Hint

Make notes in your test booklet to help you solve problems.

TEST TIME: Show Your Work

An a la carte menu charges by the
item instead of including side dishes in a meal. Cheyenne ordered
meatloaf, mashed potatoes, and a vegetable. How much
was the total for her order?

Item	Cost
Chicken or ham	$3.50
Meatloaf	$3.25
Potatoes—mashed, baked, or homefries	$2.25
Vegetable	$1.25
Soup	$1.25
Green salad	$1.75

Some of the information
you need to solve a
problem may be given in
a table, graph, chart, or
picture. This problem requires
you to find the cost of each
item on the table before
you can add.

		1
Solution:	Meatloaf:	$3.25
	Mashed potatoes:	$2.25
	Vegetable:	+ $1.25
		$6.75

Cheyenne's total was $6.75.

14. Decimal Subtraction

Definitions

decimal numbers: Numbers that include a decimal point. Usually these are just called decimals.

decimal fractions: Decimals that have a value less than one. Decimal fractions have a zero in the ones place. For example, 0.8 is a decimal fraction.

mixed decimals: Decimals that have a value greater than one. Mixed decimals have digits other than zero on both sides of the decimal point. For example, 2.5 is a mixed decimal.

Subtracting by Place Value

Subtract 0.75 − 0.34

Step 1: Subtract decimals in the same way as whole numbers. Write the decimals in a column to line up the decimal points.

$$\begin{array}{r} 0.75 \\ -\ 0.34 \\ \hline \end{array}$$

Step 2: Subtract one place at a time. Begin on the right. Subtract the hundredths.

$$\begin{array}{r} 0.75 \\ -\ 0.34 \\ \hline 1 \end{array}$$

Step 3: Subtract the tenths.

$$
\begin{array}{r}
0.75 \\
-\ 0.34 \\
\hline
41
\end{array}
$$

Step 4: Write the decimal point in the answer. Subtract the ones.

$$
\begin{array}{r}
0.75 \\
-\ 0.34 \\
\hline
0.41
\end{array}
$$

TEST TIME: Show Your Work

Subtract 2.72 − 0.3

This problem has decimal numbers with different numbers of digits. Line up the decimal points carefully. You can add zeros to the right of a decimal number without changing the value.

Solution:

$$
\begin{array}{r}
2.72 \\
-\ 0.3 \\
\hline
\end{array}
\qquad
\begin{array}{r}
2.72 \\
-\ 0.30 \\
\hline
2.42
\end{array}
$$

$2.72 - 0.3 = 2.42$

Subtracting with Zeros

Subtract 10 − 7.54

Step 1: Write the decimals in a column. Add zeros to give each number the same number of decimal places.

$$
\begin{array}{r}
10.00 \\
-\ 7.54 \\
\hline
\end{array}
$$

Step 2: You must regroup before you can subtract. There are no hundredths, tenths, or ones to regroup. You can regroup 1 ten as 9 ones, 9 tenths, and 10 hundredths.

$$
\begin{array}{r}
9\ 9\,10 \\
\not1\not0.\not0\not0 \\
-\ 7.54 \\
\hline
\end{array}
$$

Step 3: Write the decimal point in the answer. Subtract in each place, from right to left. Remember to write the decimal point in the answer.

$$
\begin{array}{r}
9\ 9\,10 \\
\not1\not0.\not0\not0 \\
-\ 7.54 \\
\hline
2.46
\end{array}
$$

Test-Taking Hint

When you use a calculator, you still need to understand what to do with the numbers in the problem. A calculator is only a tool, not a problem-solver.

TEST TIME: Multiple Choice

The 60-channel cable plan costs $26.99 per month. The 90-channel plan costs $32.99 per month. With the 60-channel plan, you can pay for select additional channels for $1.99 each. The 90-channel plan lets you get those channels for $1.29 each. What is the difference in cost between the 60-channel plan with two additional channels and the 90-channel plan with one additional channel?

a. $3.31
b. $5.30
c. $6.00
d. $6.70

Before you can find the difference between the costs of the two options, you must find the cost of each option. To solve a problem like this quickly, you can use a calculator for each step.

60-channel with 2 additional: $26.99 + $1.99 + $1.99 = $30.97
90-channel with 1 additional: $32.99 + $1.29 = $34.28
The difference is found by subtracting. $34.28 − $30.97 = $3.31

Solution: The correct answer is a.

15. Integer Addition

Definitions

whole numbers: The numbers 0, 1, 2, 3, 4, 5, . . . (and so on).

integers: Whole numbers and their opposites.

absolute value: The distance a number is from zero on a number line. Distance is always a positive value, so absolute value is always positive. The symbol for the absolute value of a number is vertical lines around the number, as in $|3|$.

Like Integers

Integers that have the same sign (positive or negative) are called like integers.

What is the sum of $^+4 + {}^+1$?

Step 1: Positive integers are normally written without the positive sign. Write the problem without the positive signs.

$$4 + 1$$

Step 2: Add.

$$4 + 1 = 5$$

Step 3: Since the problem uses the positive sign, put the sign in the answer.

$$^+4 + {}^+1 = {}^+5$$

Negative Numbers

Add. $^-3 + ^-4$

Step 1: To add any like integers, add their absolute values.

$$|^-3| + |^-4| = 3 + 4 = 7$$

Step 2: Put the negative signs back in. The addends are negative, so the sum is also negative.

$$^-3 + ^-4 = ^-7$$

TEST TIME: Show Your Work

A football team's first play resulted in a 3-yard loss. Then it lost 10 more yards to a penalty. What was the overall loss?

A loss is a negative number. Add the two losses. Write the answer in a complete sentence.

Solution: $^-3 + ^-10 = ^-13$
The overall loss was 13 yards.

Unlike Integers

Integers that have different signs (positive or negative) are called unlike integers.

Add $^+4$ and $^-8$

Step 1: Use a number line to help you understand addition of unlike integers. Begin on the number line at the first addend, $^+4$.

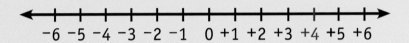

Step 2: To add a positive value on a number line, move right. To add a negative value on a number line, move left. Move left 8 units.

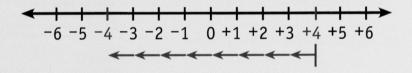

Step 3: You end at $^-4$.

$$^+4 + {}^-8 = {}^-4$$

Test-Taking Hint

Work at your own pace. Don't worry about how fast anyone else is taking the same test.

TEST TIME: Multiple Choice

What is the sum of −2 + +3?

> a. −5
>
> b. −1
>
> c. +1
>
> d. +5

The addends in this problem are unlike integers. Add unlike integers by finding the difference of their absolute values. Ignore the positive and negative signs. Subtract the smaller number from the larger.

$$|-2| = 2 \quad |+3| = 3$$
$$3 - 2 = 1$$

The final answer has the same sign as the integer with the greater absolute value. Since 3 > 2, the answer is positive.

Solution: Answer c is correct.

You can check the answer to this problem using a number line. Begin at the first addend, ⁻2. To add a positive 3, move right 3 units.

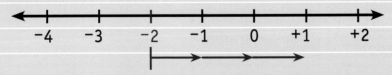

16. Integer Subtraction

Inverse Operations

Addition and subtraction are inverse operations. This allows you to subtract a number by adding the opposite.

Subtract $^{+}5 - {}^{-}8$

Step 1: To subtract integers, add the opposite. Write the first number.

$$^{+}5$$

Step 2: Change the subtraction symbol to an addition symbol.

$$^{+}5 +$$

Step 3: Write the opposite of the second number.

$$^{+}5 + {}^{+}8$$

Step 4: Add. $\qquad ^{+}5 + {}^{+}8 = {}^{+}13$

$$^{+}5 - {}^{-}8 = {}^{+}13$$

Test-Taking Hint

Watch for clue words in word problems that tell you what operation is being performed.

TEST TIME: Show Your Work

The boiling point of chloroform is 61°C. The freezing point of chloroform is ⁻63°C. What is the variation in temperature between the boiling point and freezing point of chloroform?

The word *variation* means difference, so this is a subtraction problem. You can subtract the temperatures by adding the opposite.

Solution:

If you subtract the negative from the positive you get:

$$+61 - {}^-63 = +61 + {}^+63 = +124$$

If you subtract the positive from the negative you get:

$$^-63 - {}^+61 = {}^-63 + {}^-61 = -124$$

The question is asked in a way that you should use a positive answer.

The boiling and freezing points vary by 124°C.

TEST TIME: Explain Your Answer

Explain how to add and subtract like and unlike integers.

Solution:

To add like integers ignore the positive or negative sign.
Add the numbers. The sum has the same sign as the addends.

$$+2 + +1 = +3$$
$$-2 + -1 = -3$$

To add unlike integers, ignore the positive or negative sign and find
the difference. The difference has the same sign as the greater addend.

$$-6 + +2$$
$$6 - 2 = 4, 6 > 2$$
$$-6 + +2 = -4$$

To subtract like or unlike integers, <u>add the opposite integer</u>.
Follow the rules for adding integers.

$$-9 - +5 = -9 + -5 = -14$$

Subtracting Like Integers

Subtract 12 − 20

Step 1: Numbers with no sign are positive. Both numbers in this problem are positive integers. To subtract integers, add the opposite. Write the first number.

$$^+12$$

Step 2: Change the subtraction symbol to an addition symbol.

$$^+12 \ +$$

Step 3: Write the opposite of the second number. Since 20 is positive, add a negative 20.

$$^+12 \ + \ ^-20$$

Step 4: Add. To add unlike integers, find the difference in the absolute values. Ignore the signs and subtract.

$$20 - 12 = 8$$

Find the sign of the number with the larger absolute value.

$$20 > 12$$

Since 20 is negative, the answer is negative.

$$12 - 20 = {}^-8$$

17. Fraction Addition

Definitions

denominator: The bottom number in a fraction. It tells the total number of equal parts.

numerator: The top number in a fraction. It tells the number of parts being talked about.

like fractions: Fractions that have the same denominator.

unlike fractions: Fractions that have different denominators.

Like Fractions

Add $\frac{5}{9}$ and $\frac{2}{9}$

Step 1: To add like fractions, add only the numerators, 5 and 2.

$$\frac{5}{9} + \frac{2}{9} = \frac{5 + 2}{} = \frac{7}{}$$

Step 2: Keep the same denominator, 9.

$$\frac{5}{9} + \frac{2}{9} = \frac{5 + 2}{9} = \frac{7}{9}$$

Definition

lowest terms: A fraction is in lowest terms when the numerator and denominator do not have any common factors except 1.

TEST TIME: Show Your Work

Derek spent $^1/_8$ of his savings on new tires. He spent another $^3/_8$ of savings on a new transmission. How much of his savings did Derek spend?

A fraction of Derek's savings was spent on tires and a fraction of his savings was spent on a transmission. The problem asks for the total fraction that was spent. Problems that ask for a total are often addition problems. Add the two fractions to find the answer.

Solution: $\quad\quad\quad\quad ^1/_8 + ^3/_8 = ^4/_8$

Reduce fractions to lowest terms by dividing both the numerator and denominator by the same number. Divide each by 4.

$$^4/_8 = ^1/_2$$

Write the answer in a full sentence.

Derek spent $^1/_2$ of his savings.

Definition

equivalent: Equal in value. For example, 1/2 = 2/4 = 4/8

TEST TIME: Explain Your Answer

Explain one way to find a fraction that is equivalent to 1/4.

Solution: You can multiply both the numerator and denominator by the same number without changing the value of a fraction. This is one way to find an equivalent fraction.

$$\frac{1}{4} = \frac{1 \times 2 = 2}{4 \times 2 = 8}$$

The fraction 2/8 is equivalent to 1/4.

Unlike Fractions

Unlike fractions are written as like fractions before they are added. Write equivalent fractions for each addend, so that the denominators of the addends are the same.

Add 1/6 and 3/4

Step 1: Write unlike fractions as like fractions using the least common denominator. Find the least common multiple of the denominators, 6 and 4.

List the multiples of 6: 6, 12, 18, 24, . . .
List the multiples of 4: 4, 8, 12, 16, 20, . . .
The least common multiple of 6 and 4 is 12.

Write both fractions with a denominator of 12.

$$\frac{1}{6} = \frac{1 \times 2}{6 \times 2} = \frac{2}{12} \qquad\qquad \frac{3}{4} = \frac{3 \times 3}{4 \times 3} = \frac{9}{12}$$

Step 2: Write the problem using the equivalent like fractions.

$$\frac{1}{6} + \frac{3}{4} \quad \text{is the same as} \quad \frac{2}{12} + \frac{9}{12}$$

Step 3: Add.

$$\frac{2}{12} + \frac{9}{12} = \frac{2 + 9}{12} = \frac{11}{12}$$

18. Mixed Fraction Addition

Definitions

proper fraction: A fraction whose numerator is less than its denominator. Example: 4/9

improper fraction: A fraction whose numerator is equal to or greater than its denominator. Example: 8/5 or 5/5

mixed fraction: A number made of two parts: a whole number and a proper fraction. Mixed fractions are also called mixed numbers. Example: $2 \frac{1}{3}$

Like Mixed Fractions

Add 3 $\frac{2}{5}$ and 1 $\frac{2}{5}$

Step 1: Add the fractions.　　　　　$\frac{2}{5} + \frac{2}{5} = \frac{4}{5}$

Step 2: Add the whole numbers.　　　$3 + 1 = 4$

Step 3: Add the whole number sum　$4 + + \frac{4}{5} = 4\frac{4}{5}$
and the fraction sum.

Test-Taking Hint

Be careful to avoid careless answers on easy questions. Focus on each problem, and don't be in a hurry.

Sarah used 2 $\frac{2}{3}$ cups of sugar to make cookies. She used another 4 $\frac{2}{3}$ cups to make icing. How much sugar did Sarah use in all?

a. 6 $\frac{1}{3}$ cups
b. 7 $\frac{1}{3}$ cups
c. 7 $\frac{2}{3}$ cups
d. 7 $\frac{4}{3}$ cups

To find a combined amount, add the mixed fractions.
The fraction sum is an improper fraction. Regroup the sum of the fraction parts as a mixed fraction.

2 $\frac{2}{3}$ + 4 $\frac{2}{3}$

Fraction parts:	$\frac{2}{3} + \frac{2}{3} = \frac{4}{3} = 1 \frac{1}{3}$
Whole number parts:	$2 + 4 = 6$
Combined sum:	$1 \frac{1}{3} + 6 = 7 \frac{1}{3}$

Solution: Answer b is correct.

Unlike Mixed Fractions

Add 2 1/3 and 4 1/6

Step 1: Write the problem using like fractions. Look at the denominators. How can you change 1/3 to a fraction with a denominator of 6? Multiply by 2.

$$\frac{1}{3} = \frac{1 \times 2}{3 \times 2} = \frac{2}{6}$$

2 1/3 + 4 1/6 **is the same as** 2 2/6 + 4 1/6

Step 2: Add the fractions. $2/6 + 1/6 = 3/6$

Step 3: Reduce the fraction to lowest terms. Both 3 and 6 are divisible by 3.

$$\frac{3}{6} = \frac{3 \div 3}{6 \div 3} = \frac{1}{2}$$

Step 4: Add the whole numbers. $2 + 4 = 6$

Step 5: Add the whole number sum $6 + 1/2 = 6\,1/2$
and the fraction sum.

Test-Taking Hint

Some multiple choice questions can be solved by eliminating choices that are obviously incorrect.

TEST TIME: Multiple Choice

Meghan started reading a book on Monday. On Monday, she read 3 $\frac{1}{5}$ chapters. On Tuesday, she read another 3 $\frac{1}{4}$ chapters. How many chapters had Meghan read by Tuesday night?

a. 5 $\frac{9}{20}$
b. 6 $\frac{1}{5}$
c. 6 $\frac{1}{9}$
d. 6 $\frac{9}{20}$

You can eliminate answer a immediately by understanding that Meghan read more than 3 chapters each day, so her total for both days is greater than 6. Answers b and c may also be quickly eliminated by knowing addition of the fraction part is $\frac{1}{5} + \frac{1}{4}$. Answer b adds the whole numbers, but only includes one of the fraction parts. Answer c adds the whole numbers, but the fraction part is less than either of the fraction parts in the two addends. The only answer left is answer d.

Solution: Answer d is correct.

You can check the answer to this problem by doing the addition. Write 3 $\frac{1}{5}$ and 3 $\frac{1}{4}$ using the least common denominator, 20, then add.

$$3 \tfrac{1}{5} + 3 \tfrac{1}{4} = 3 \tfrac{4}{20} + 3 \tfrac{5}{20} = 6 \tfrac{9}{20}$$

19. Fraction Subtraction

Subtracting Like Fractions

Find the difference between 13/16 and 5/16.

Step 1: To subtract like fractions, subtract only the numerators.

$$\frac{13}{16} - \frac{5}{16} = \frac{13 - 5}{} = \frac{8}{}$$

Step 2: Keep the same denominator.

$$\frac{13}{16} - \frac{5}{16} = \frac{13 - 5}{16} = \frac{8}{16}$$

Step 3: Reduce to lowest terms.

$$\frac{8}{16} = \frac{1}{2}$$

Test-Taking Hint

Write fractions in your answers in lowest terms.

TEST TIME: Show Your Work

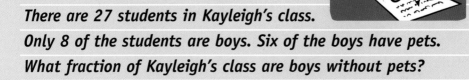

There are 27 students in Kayleigh's class.
Only 8 of the students are boys. Six of the boys have pets.
What fraction of Kayleigh's class are boys without pets?

This problem can be solved in more than one way.
Write the number of boys in Kayleigh's class as a fraction.
Write the number of boys in Kayleigh's class with pets as
a fraction.Subtract to find the fraction of the class that are
boys without pets.

Solution: 8 out of 27 students are boys, or 8/27.
6 out of 27 students are boys with pets, or 6/27.

$$8/27 - 6/27 = 2/27$$

2/27 of Kayleigh's class are boys without pets.

Another way to solve this problem is to find the number of boys
without pets. There are 8 boys, and 6 have pets.
8 − 6 = 2 boys without pets.
Write 2 out of 27 as the fraction 2/27.

Unlike Fractions

Unlike fractions are subtracted in the same way as they are added. Change the fractions first, so that the denominators are the same.

Subtract 7/8 − 1/2

Step 1: Write unlike fractions as like fractions using the least common denominator. Find the least common multiple of the denominators, 2 and 8.

> List the multiples of 2: 2, 4, 6, 8, 10, 12, . . .
> List the multiples of 8: 8, 16, 24, 32, . . .
> Least common multiple of 2 and 8: 8

Write each fraction with a denominator of 8.

$$\frac{1}{2} = \frac{1 \times 4}{2 \times 4} = \frac{4}{8} \qquad\qquad \frac{7}{8} = \frac{7}{8}$$

Step 2: Write the problem using the like fractions.

$$\frac{7}{8} - \frac{4}{8}$$

Step 3: Subtract.

$$\frac{7}{8} - \frac{4}{8} = \frac{3}{8}$$

$$\frac{7}{8} - \frac{1}{2} = \frac{3}{8}$$

TEST TIME: Multiple Choice

Which of the following is NOT correct?

$$\text{a. } 7/12 - 1/3 = 1/4$$
$$\text{b. } 2/3 - 1/2 = 1/6$$
$$\text{c. } 3/5 - 3/10 = 1/2$$
$$\text{d. } 5/8 - 1/4 = 3/8$$

This problem asks you to find the equation that is not correct. Three of the four ARE correct. None of these answers is easy to eliminate.

One way to solve this problem is to solve each equation. Remember, you are looking for the equation that is NOT correct.

a. $7/12 - 1/3 = 7/12 - 4/12 = 3/12 = 1/4$

b. $2/3 - 1/2 = 4/6 - 3/6 = 1/6$

c. $3/5 - 3/10 = 6/10 - 3/10 = 3/10$

d. $5/8 - 1/4 = 5/8 - 2/8 = 3/8$

Solution: The only equation that is not correct is in answer c.

20. Mixed Fraction Subtraction

TEST TIME: Show Your Work

Subtract 8 9/10 − 4 2/10

First subtract the fraction parts.
Then subtract the whole number parts.

Solution:

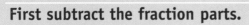

8 9/10	8 9/10	8 9/10
− 4 2/10	− 4 2/10	− 4 2/10
	7/10	4 7/10

8 9/10 − 4 2/10 = 4 7/10

Test-Taking Hint

Mixed fractions, as well as fractions, should always be reduced to lowest terms. Both answers are correct, but an answer in lowest terms is better.

Regrouping Mixed Fractions

Mixed fractions may need to be regrouped before they can be subtracted.

Stan's foot is 9 1/6 inches long. Liz's foot is 6 5/6 inches long. How much longer is Stan's foot than Liz's?

Step 1: Use subtraction to find the difference in the number of inches. The numerator 5 is greater than the numerator 1. Regroup the whole number 9 as $8\,^6/_6$.

$$9\,^1/_6 = 8 + {}^6/_6 + {}^1/_6 = \quad 8\,^7/_6$$
$$-\ 6\,^5/_6 \qquad\qquad\qquad\qquad -\ 6\,^5/_6$$

Step 2: Subtract.

$$8\,^7/_6$$
$$-\ 6\,^5/_6$$
$$\overline{2\,^2/_6}$$

Step 3: Reduce to lowest terms.

$$2\,^2/_6 = 2\,^1/_3$$

Stan's foot is $2\,^1/_3$ inches longer than Liz's foot.

TEST TIME: Show Your Work

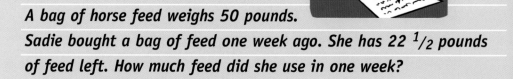

A bag of horse feed weighs 50 pounds.
Sadie bought a bag of feed one week ago. She has 22 $\frac{1}{2}$ pounds
of feed left. How much feed did she use in one week?

Whole numbers can be written as mixed fractions.
Regroup 50 pounds so that one pound is written as an
improper fraction with a denominator of 2.

Solution:

Full bag of feed — amount left = amount used

50 lbs — 22 $\frac{1}{2}$ lbs = amount used

50 = 49 $\frac{2}{2}$

Subtract the fraction part.

Subtract whole number part.

$$49 \tfrac{2}{2}$$
$$- \; 22 \tfrac{1}{2}$$
$$\overline{27 \tfrac{1}{2}}$$

Sadie used 27 $\frac{1}{2}$ pounds of feed in one week.

Test-Taking Hint

Most tests are scored on the number of questions you
answer correctly. You do not lose points for wrong
answers. Answer every question, even if you have to guess.

Unlike Mixed Fractions

Subtract $2\,5/6 - 1\,1/3$

Step 1: Write the problem using like fractions.

$$\begin{array}{r} 2\,5/6 \\ -\ 1\,1/3 \\ \hline \end{array} \qquad \begin{array}{r} 2\,5/6 \\ -\ 1\,2/6 \\ \hline \end{array}$$

Step 2: Subtract the fractions.

$$\begin{array}{r} 2\,5/6 \\ -\ 1\,2/6 \\ \hline 3/6 \end{array}$$

Step 3: Subtract the whole numbers.

$$\begin{array}{r} 2\,5/6 \\ -\ 1\,2/6 \\ \hline 1\,3/6 \end{array}$$

Step 4: Reduce the fraction to lowest terms. $1\,3/6 = 1\,1/2$

21. Adding Measurements

Like Units

Measurements that have like units are added like any other values.

Add 215 gallons and 57 gallons.

Step 1: The units are both gallons. Line up the numbers in a column by their place value.

$$
\begin{array}{r}
215 \\
+\ \ 57 \\
\hline
\end{array}
$$

Step 2: Add from right to left.

$$
\begin{array}{r}
1\ \ \ \\
215 \\
+\ \ 57 \\
\hline
272 \\
\end{array}
$$

Step 3: Always include measurement units in the answer when they are given in the problem.

215 gallons + 57 gallons = 272 gallons

TEST TIME: Explain Your Answer

Explain how to convert measurements within a system (length, weight, time).

Solution: To convert from a larger unit to a smaller unit, use multiplication. For example, to convert from feet to inches, multiply by the number of inches in one foot, 12.

1 foot: 1 × 12 = 12 inches
2 feet: 2 × 12 = 24 inches
3 feet: 3 × 12 = 36 inches

To convert from a smaller unit to a larger unit, use division. For example, to convert from feet to yards, divide by the number of feet in one yard, 3.

3 feet: 3 ÷ 3 = 1 yard
6 feet: 6 ÷ 3 = 2 yards
9 feet: 9 ÷ 3 = 3 yards

Length

There are 2 feet of tape left on one roll. A second roll has 60 inches of tape. How much tape is on the two rolls together?

Step 1: Add only like units. This problem does not tell you what unit the answer should be in. You can choose to use inches or feet. Let's use inches. Convert feet to inches by multiplying by 12.

Roll 1:   2 feet = 24 inches
Roll 2:   60 inches

Step 2: Add the inches.

$$\begin{aligned} 24 \text{ inches} \\ + \ 60 \text{ inches} \\ \hline 84 \text{ inches} \end{aligned}$$

There are 84 inches of tape on the two rolls.

Let's see what happens when we use feet. Convert inches to feet by dividing by 12.

Roll 1:   2 feet
Roll 2:   60 inches = 5 feet

2 feet + 5 feet = 7 feet

There are 7 feet of tape on the two rolls.

Both answers are correct because 7 feet = 84 inches.

TEST TIME: Multiple Choice

A triangle has side lengths of 3 meters, 4.2 meters, and 2.7 meters. What is the perimeter of the triangle?

   a. 7.2 meters
   b. 9.9 meters
   c. 6.9 meters
   d. 9.7 meters

The perimeter of a triangle is the total distance around the triangle. To find the perimeter, add the three side lengths of the triangle.

$$
\begin{array}{r}
3.0 \text{ meters} \\
4.2 \text{ meters} \\
+\ 2.7 \text{ meters} \\
\hline
9.9 \text{ meters}
\end{array}
$$

Solution: Answer b is correct.

Test-Taking Hint
Know math definitions. The words used on tests are ones that you should already be familiar with.

22. Subtracting Measurements

Weight

Measurements that have like units are subtracted like any other values.

Jill's cat weighs 16 pounds 8 ounces. Her new puppy weighs 6 pounds 2 ounces. How much more does her cat weigh than her puppy?

Step 1: This problem asks for the difference in weight. It is a subtraction problem. The weights for both animals are given in pounds and ounces. Line up the like values.

Cat   16 pounds 8 ounces
Puppy   − 6 pounds 2 ounces

Step 2: Subtract pounds from pounds and ounces from ounces.

Cat   16 pounds 8 ounces
Puppy   − 6 pounds 2 ounces
                 10 pounds 6 ounces

The cat weighs 10 pounds 6 ounces more than the puppy.

Test-Taking Hint

Know your calculator. If you're using someone else's calculator, make sure you understand how to use it before you begin a test.

TEST TIME: Multiple Choice

Lauren drove 18,754.3 miles on business trips last year. This year she drove 27,074.1 miles. How much farther did she drive on business trips this year than she did last year?

a. 8,320.2 miles

b. 8,420.8 miles

c. 8,319.8 miles

d. 9,319.8 miles

Subtract using either a calculator or a paper and pencil. Large numbers or numbers that require regrouping in more than one place can be done quickly on a calculator.

$$27{,}074.1 - 18{,}754.3 = 8{,}319.8$$

Solution: The correct answer is c.

Time

On a senior project, Jarrod spent 1 week and 6 days in Bolivia and another 2 weeks and 2 days in Chile. How much longer was he in Chile than in Bolivia?

Step 1: Subtract only like units. Weeks are subtracted from weeks, and days are subtracted from days. Write the problem in a column. Line up the units that are the same.

Chile: 2 weeks and 2 days
Bolivia: − 1 week and 6 days

Step 2: Regroup to subtract days. 1 week is the same as 7 days. Regroup 2 weeks and 2 days as 1 week and 9 days.

$$
\begin{array}{r}
1 \qquad\quad 9 \\
\cancel{2}\ \text{weeks and}\ \cancel{2}\ \text{days} \\
-\ 1\ \text{week}\ \ \text{and}\ \ 6\ \text{days} \\
\hline
3\ \text{days}
\end{array}
$$

Step 3: There are no weeks left after subtracting.

$$
\begin{array}{r}
1 \qquad\quad 9 \\
\cancel{2}\ \text{weeks and}\ \cancel{2}\ \text{days} \\
-\ 1\ \text{week}\ \ \text{and}\ \ 6\ \text{days} \\
\hline
3\ \text{days}
\end{array}
$$

Jarrod spent 3 days longer in Chile than he did in Bolivia.

TEST TIME: Show Your Work

*Find the difference in centimeters
between 3 meters and 52 centimeters.*

Metric units are related to each other by powers of 10. A meter is the same length as 10 decimeters, or 100 centimeters. Convert meters to centimeters by multiplying by 100.

Solution:

3 meters	300 centimeters
− 52 centimeters	− 52 centimeters
	248 centimeters

The difference between 3 meters and 52 centimeters is 248 centimeters.

Test-Taking Hint

You can go through a test and do the easy problems first. This can help you gain confidence and keeps you from running out of time and missing easy points.

23. Estimation: Addition

Definition

estimate: An answer that is not exact. A good estimate is an answer that is close to the exact answer.

Rounding

Howie has $4,985 in his savings account and $1,119 in his checking account. About how much does Howie have in the two accounts?

Step 1: This problem does not ask for an exact answer. Estimate the combined total by rounding each number, then adding. Round each number to the nearest thousands place.

$4,985 rounds to $5,000
$1,119 rounds to $1,000

Step 2: Use mental math to add.

$5,000 + $1,000 = $6,000

Howie has about $6,000 in his two accounts.

Test-Taking Hint

When you estimate, the answer is not exact. Include words such as about or around in your answer.

TEST TIME: Multiple Choice

Which of the following is NOT a good reason to estimate?

a. Because you don't need an exact answer.
b. To predict what the answer might be.
c. Because you don't want to solve the problem.
d. To check if an answer is reasonable.

This problem asks you to decide which reason is NOT a good one to find an estimate.

When you don't need an exact answer, to predict the answer, and to check if your answer is reasonable are all good reasons to estimate. To estimate because you don't want to solve a problem is NOT a good reason to estimate.

Solution: The correct answer is c.

Test-Taking Hint

Rounding a number closer to the original number will result in an estimated answer that is closer to the exact answer.

Estimate Fractions

One way to estimate the answer to a problem that uses fractions is to use fractions that work well together. For example, like fractions are easy to add and subtract.

Estimate the sum of 1/8, 1/7, and 1/9.

Step 1: 1/7 and 1/9 are both close to 1/8. 1/8 is one of the addends. Change 1/7 to 1/8 and 1/9 to 1/8.

$$\frac{1}{7} + \frac{1}{8} + \frac{1}{9} \text{ is close to } \frac{1}{8} + \frac{1}{8} + \frac{1}{8}$$

Step 2: Use mental math.

$$\frac{1}{8} + \frac{1}{8} + \frac{1}{8} = \frac{3}{8}$$

$$\frac{1}{7} + \frac{1}{8} + \frac{1}{9} \text{ is about } \frac{3}{8}$$

TEST TIME: Show Your Work

Alexander wants to buy a hockey ticket
for $87.50, a hat for $13.99, and a team jersey for $67.50.
If he has $180, does he have enough money to buy all of the items?

To make sure you have enough of something, you can round all of the values up to the next whole dollar, then estimate. This is a high estimate, but you will be sure you have enough money.

Solution: $87.50 + $13.99 + $67.50
                    $88 + $14 + $68 = $170

A high estimate of the cost is $170, and Alexander has $180.
He should have enough money to buy all of the items.

Test-Taking Hint

Make sure you are answering the question that is asked. Some problems require more than one step. In the problem above you must estimate the total cost, then compare the estimate to the amount Alexander has to spend.

24. Estimation: Subtraction

Estimating with Decimals

You can estimate with decimals by rounding the decimals to a whole number or to a set place value.

Subtract 9.7 − 3.8. Estimate to check the answer.

Step 1: Line up the decimals by place value. Subtract.

$$
\begin{array}{r}
\overset{8\ 17}{\cancel{9.7}} \\
-\ 3.8 \\
\hline
5.9
\end{array}
$$

Step 2: Round each decimal to the nearest whole number.

9.7 rounds to 10

3.8 rounds to 4

Step 3: Subtract the rounded numbers.

10 − 4 = 6

5.9 is very close to 6.

Test-Taking Hint

Use estimation to check the results of exact answers.

TEST TIME: Explain Your Answer

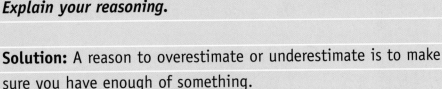

Give examples of when you might choose to overestimate and underestimate. Explain your reasoning.

Solution: A reason to overestimate or underestimate is to make sure you have enough of something.

You might choose to underestimate the amount of time you have to spend doing something. For example, you might think, I have 10 minutes to get ready, when the exact amount of time you have is 13 minutes. This way, if you take a minute or two longer, you are still on time.

You might choose to overestimate the amount of paper you need to print a project. By overestimating, you can be more sure that you have enough paper, instead of running out.

Definition

greatest place value: The first place from the left in a number that has a digit other than zero. For example, in the number 0.014, the first digit from the left that is not zero is the 1 in the hundredths place.

Greatest Place Value

Use rounding to the greatest place value to estimate 26.79 − 21.01. Is this a good estimate? How can you find a better estimate?

Step 1: Round each number to its greatest place value. The greatest place value in each number is the tens place.

26.79 rounded to the tens place is 30.
21.01 rounded to the tens place is 20.

Step 2: Subtract the rounded numbers.

$$30 - 20 = 10$$

Step 3: Let's use a calculator to find the exact answer.

26.79 − 21.01 = 5.78

This is not a very good estimate.

Step 4: Try rounding to the nearest whole number.

26.79 rounded to the ones place is 27.
21.01 rounded to the ones place is 21.

Step 5: Subtract the rounded numbers.

$$27 - 21 = 6$$

6 is close to the exact answer of 5.78. You can get a better estimate by rounding to the ones place than you do when you round to the tens place.

TEST TIME: Show Your Work

Shelly has 172 feet of lights to decorate her house for the holidays. She wants to run 226 feet of lights on the border of her roof. Use compatible numbers to estimate the number of feet of lights that Shelly still needs.

Compatible numbers are numbers that work well together. Choose numbers that are close to the original problem but that you can use to subtract mentally. Multiples of 25 are often ones that people are familiar with.

Solution: $226 - 172$ is about $225 - 175$
$$225 - 175 = 50$$

Shelly still needs about 50 more feet of lights.

Further Reading

Books

McKellar, Danica. *Math Doesn't Suck: How to Survive Middle School Math Without Losing Your Mind or Breaking a Nail.* New York: Hudson Street Press, 2007.

Rozakis, Laurie. *Get Test Smart! The Ultimate Guide to Middle School Standardized Tests.* New York: Scholastic Reference, 2007.

Yoder, Eric, and Natalie Yoder. *65 Short Mysteries You Solve With Math!* Washington, DC: Science, Naturally! 2010.

Internet Addresses

Banfill, J. **AAA Math.** 2009.
http://www.aaastudy.com/add.htm
http://www.aaastudy.com/sub.htm

Drexel University. **Ask Dr. Math.** 1994–2011.
http://mathforum.org/library/drmath/sets/elem_addition.html
http://mathforum.org/library/drmath/sets/elem_subtraction.html

TestTakingTips.com. **Test Taking Tips.** 2003–2011.
http://www.testtakingtips.com/test/math.htm

Index